Microeconomics for Students & Managers
Rapid Introduction & Review

Author's Note

With virtually unlimited access to online lecture videos, notes and discussion forums, learning has been revolutionized over the past decade. While on one hand, seeking knowledge has become easier; seeking the right topic or information, in the presence of so many options, can sometimes be overwhelming or time consuming.

There has never been more need for books that can be used for quick reference or rapid learning. Such books not only introduce with the basic concepts, but also make learning more efficient and encourage to delve further into the subject.

"Microeconomics for Students & Managers" is the first book of the series. Every effort has been made to keep it short, concise and easy to browse without skipping key concepts. Hopefully it becomes a good source of learning and reference for students and professionals alike.

Fraz Tajammul

Contents

Introduction

- Economics is a social science that mainly deals with the description and analysis of production, distribution and consumption of goods and services. It defines the principles of efficient allocation of scarce resources.

Economic Resources

- Economic resources are the inputs that are used to create goods or services.

  Land is an economic resource. This also includes natural resources (water, fossil fuels, minerals etc.) that come from the land. While some of the natural resources (e.g. timber) are renewable, land itself is a fixed resource as well as fossil fuels and minerals.

  Labor is the effort (mental and physical) that people contribute to the production of goods or services. It is a flexible resource. Human capital is the measure of ability (skill, education, experience etc.) of workers to perform labor.

  Capital is the physical asset that has been produced and is used to produce goods or services, e.g. production facilities and equipment etc. are considered capital.

  Entrepreneurship is also considered a factor of production. Entrepreneur is an individual that uses economic resources and transforms them into goods and services, and assumes all risks and rewards.

- Energy is considered a secondary factor of production as it is obtained from land, labor and capital.
- Money is not considered a factor of production. It is not a productive resource as it cannot be used to create goods or services. It is rather a resource that facilitates acquisition of factors of production.

Markets & Circular Flow Model

- Market is an actual or nominal place where buyers and sellers of a good or service interact to facilitate an exchange.

Product Markets

- Product market is the place where final (finished) goods and services are offered for purchase, e.g. pharmaceutical market, market for cars and market for financial services such as banks etc.
- Households are the main buyers of products and services in product markets.

Resource Markets

- These are the markets where factors of production are bought and sold, e.g. labor market is a resource market that deals with the interaction of workers and employers.
Firms purchase resources from households in resource (factor) markets to produce goods and services.

Circular Flow Model

- Federal, state and local governments focus on maintaining economic stability and facilitating systems that generate economic activities. Governments make purchases, collect taxes from firms and households, offer subsidies etc.

- A simplified circular flow model is shown below. Primary components in this model are households, firms and government.

- This model illustrates how goods and services are exchanged in product and factor markets.

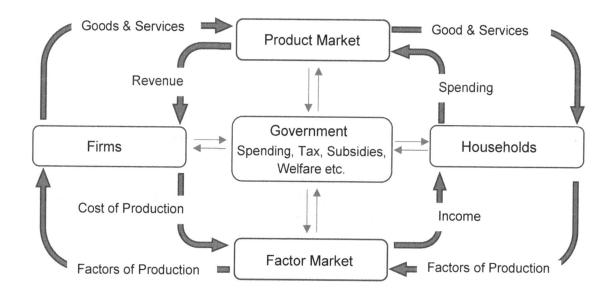

Microeconomics & Macroeconomics

- Economics can be divided in two categories:
  - Microeconomics
  - Macroeconomics

- Microeconomics is a branch of economics that examines the behavior of basic elements (households and firms) in economy, and their interactions.

It discusses conditions under which markets lead to desirable allocations and analyzes mechanisms that establish prices of goods and services. It also deals with the causes and effects of economic policies (e.g. taxation, subsidies) and inefficient allocation of resources (market failure).

- Macroeconomics is the study of entire economy and related policies using aggregated indicators such as GDP, inflation, price indexes, national income, unemployment rates etc. It also develops models that explain relationships between these indicators.

Economic Systems

- Economic systems are classified based on their dominant characteristics as they rarely exist in pure form. These are complex systems so the following descriptions are not complete.

Capitalism:

- In pure capitalism, individuals and businesses work in their own interest and maximize profit whereas, government does not interfere in the market.
- Capitalism is therefore based on private ownership of factors of production, and allocation of resources is based on law of demand and supply.

Communism

- In this system, every resource is owned by the community and everyone in community is considered both the owner of factors of production and the employee. Benefits are distributed according to everyone's needs.
- Pure communist society has no government, decisions are made by the community and all class distinctions are eliminated.

Socialism:

- In a purely socialist system, the state owns and operates factors of production. There is no competition and all economic activities are planned by a central authority.
- It focusses on maximizing individual welfare for all persons based on needs, and also on contributions.

- These systems are not mutually exclusive as different elements of these system are found in all societies.

Elements of socialism exist with democratic political system in Scandinavian countries, Denmark, Norway, Sweden. These countries are known as social democracies.
United States is a capitalist country with relatively free markets, however public schools, social security etc. are the elements of socialism.

Chapter 01: Scarcity, Price & Allocation

Scarcity, Price & Opportunity Cost

- ***Scarcity*** means that human desire for goods, services and resources exceed what is available. Therefore, we need some form of resource allocation mechanism.
  In a free market economy, resources are allocated through interaction of market forces between consumers and producers.

- ***Prices*** act as rationing devices. Price of a good or service moves up and down depending on scarcity. It is usually the most efficient but not the only way of allocation, e.g. lottery is another allocation mechanism.
  Prices are formed by interaction of 2 parties i.e. buyers and sellers (as well as government intervention).

- ***Opportunity Cost*** means that something else has been sacrificed or given-up when a choice is made. It is the value of next best forgone opportunity. There is always a next best alternative, therefore there is always an opportunity cost.
  If a business man runs his business from the building he owns, the opportunity cost includes the amount of rent he could get by renting the place.

Demand Curve

- It is a graph, depicting relationship between the price of a good or service and the quantity that consumers are willing to purchase.
- Demand curve usually slopes downwards from left to right.
- The slope is also referred to as "***Law of Demand***" which means, if all other factors remain equal, people will buy more of a product or service if prices fall.
- This formulation implies that price is an independent variable and demand is a dependent variable.

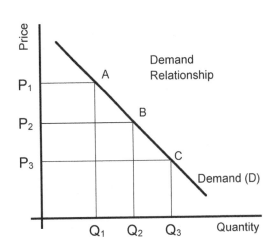

Shift vs Movement Along a Demand Curve

- Movement along demand curve occurs when change in price causes the demand to change. This happens only when the price changes.

- Shift of a demand curve takes place when a nonprice determinant results in shifting the curve (right or left).
- Factors like increase in income, preference or population size can result in increase in demand of a specific product or service and shift its demand curve to the right & vice versa.

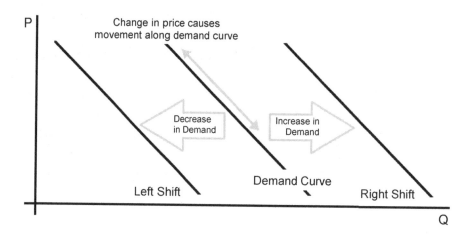

Supply Curve

- Supply curve is the relationship between the price of a good or service and the quantity producers are willing to supply.
- This curve usually slopes upwards from right to left.
- The slope is referred to as "*Law of Supply*" which means as the price of a given product increases, producers supply more quantities, all else being equal.
- This formulation implies that price is an independent variable and supply is a dependent variable.

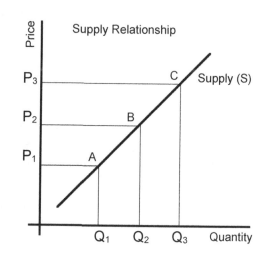

Shift vs Movement Along a Supply Curve

- Movements along supply curve occur only if there is a change in quantity supplied caused by a change in the good's own price.
- A shift in the supply curve occurs when a non-price determinant of supply changes.
  For example, if the price of an ingredient, used to produce the good increase, the supply curve would shift towards left.
- Subsidy provided by government, to producers to encourage production, shifts the supply curve to the right by the amount of subsidy.
- Technological improvements (e.g. in the field of agriculture, electronics etc.) result in more efficient production and cause the curve to shift right.

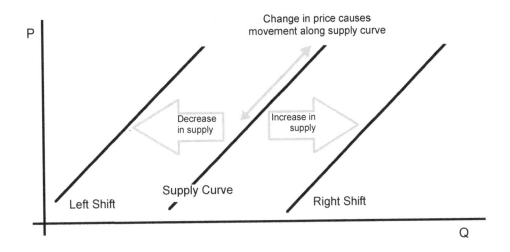

- **_Market supply curve_** is derived by summing the quantities of a product all suppliers are willing to produce when it can be sold for a given price.
- The concept of supply and demand is also applicable to different types of resource markets. Households are the suppliers of jobs whereas the firm hiring workers are the ones who demand in labor market. A higher salary means increase in the supply of labor and decrease in its demand. Resource markets have been discussed in Chapter 10 and 11 in more detail.

Equilibrium

- Equilibrium is achieved when supply and demand are equal. It is the intersection of supply and demand function.
- As shown in image (i), allocation of goods at price P^* is most efficient: the quantity of goods Q^* being supplied equals the amount of goods being demanded.

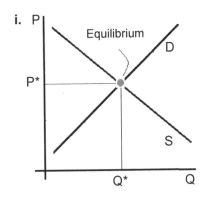
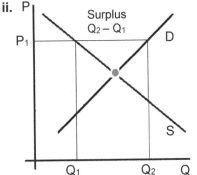
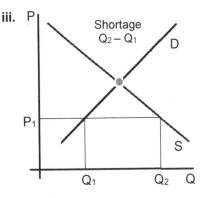

- As shown in image ii and iii, the other points on supply and demand curve represent either surplus or shortage which results in inefficient allocation. This happens when price changes and the nonprice determinant factors remain unchanged. It has been discussed in detail in the next chapter.

Shifts in Supply-Demand Curves & Equilibrium

- Increase in demand (due to nonprice factors) causes the demand curve to shift right. New equilibrium point is achieved with higher prices of the product.

- Decrease in demand causes the demand curve to shift left. This results in new equilibrium point with lower prices of the product.

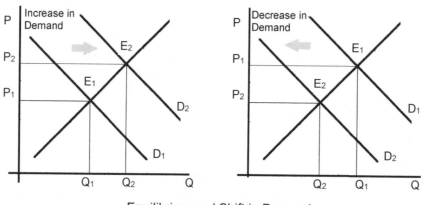

Equilibrium and Shift in Demand

- Increase in supply (due to nonprice factors) causes the supply curve to shift right. New equilibrium point is achieved with lower prices and more quantities supplied.

- Decrease in supply causes the supply curve to shift left which results in new equilibrium point with lower prices and lower quantities supplied.

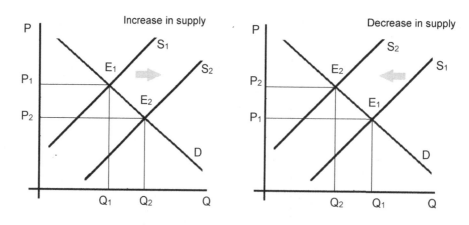

Equilibrium and Shift in Supply

Chapter 02: Price Control

- There are two ways government intervenes market for price control:
  - Direct Price Control
  - Indirect Price Control

- Direct price control is price ceiling or price floor.
- Indirect price control can be taxes or subsidies.

Price Floor

- Price floor is the minimum price of a product or service that can be charged. An **effective** (or binding) **price floor** is the one that is set above equilibrium price.

  Example:

- *P* & Q** is the free market equilibrium price and quantity of a product.

- Government sets price floor P_F of this product which is above equilibrium price. This will result in product surplus. There will be Q_D demand for the product in the market but the supply is going to be Q_S.

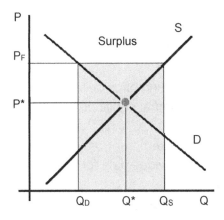

$$Surplus \ = \ Q_S \ - \ Q_D$$

- This surplus can then be purchased by the government (cost is shown by the shaded area), e.g. US government in past has purchased additional wheat from market for African countries to alleviate famine.

$$Gov.\,Purchase \ = \ P_F \ * \ (Q_S - Q_D)$$

- There can be multiple reasons for setting price floor e.g. government may decide that a product is too important and if price goes down a certain threshold suppliers may stop producing it.
- It should be noted that setting price floor below equilibrium price has no impact on market and original equilibrium point retains its position.

- Price floor is also known as **price support**. It is common in agriculture sector. Setting minimum wage is an example of price floor as well.

Price Ceiling

Price ceiling is the maximum price that can be charged. An **effective** (or binding) **price ceiling** is the one that is set below equilibrium price.

Example:

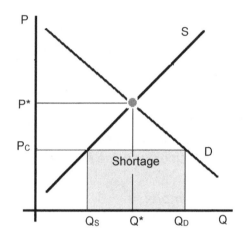

- In absence of any price control, there are Q^* apartments demanded & supplied at P^* rent. City government decides that the rents are too high and fixes prices at P_C.

- At this lower price, consumers are now going to demand Q_D apartments but suppliers are only willing to supply Q_S apartments.

- There will be shortage of apartments in the market at this price.

$$Shortage = Q_D - Q_S$$

- Consumers, who manage to find an apartment at this lower price, gain; however, producers and other consumers (who are unable to find apartments for rent) lose out.

- Setting price ceiling above equilibrium price does not impact market and prices retain at the original equilibrium point.

- Government may use price ceiling when it believes prices are too high for consumers. It provides gain for buyers and a loss for sellers.

- Capping of Swiss Franc in past is another example of price ceiling.

Indirect Price Control

- Taxation is one of the indirect price control methods.
- Subsidy, opposite to tax, is a benefit to producers or buyers with an aim of promoting economic or social benefit. It can be given in the form of financial aid or refunds, known as rebates, e.g. tax rebates.

Example of Taxation

- As shown in image, if price of gas is currently $2 per gallon and $1 tax is added, supply curve S_o will shift by $1 & new curve will be S_1. Demand curve will remain the same.

- New equilibrium point E_1 (after supply curve shift) shows that the new price does not go up by whole $1. Instead, introduction of tax causes the supply and demand quantities to decrease which results in price increase of less than $1.

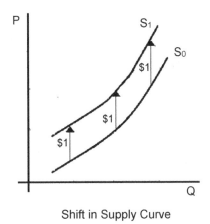

Shift in Supply Curve

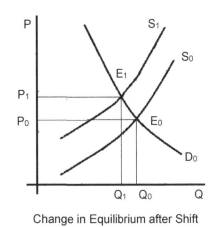

Change in Equilibrium after Shift

Incidence of Taxation

- Incidence of Taxation means "what share of tax is paid by consumers and suppliers". This share depends on the shape of demand curve.

- Consider two markets with different demand curves for gasoline but similar supply curves, S_0. Demand curve in image (i) is steeper than the one in image (ii).
  Gasoline price is $2 in both markets before tax. Same tax ($1) levied on both markets shifts supply curves to S_1 and results in different incidence of taxation.

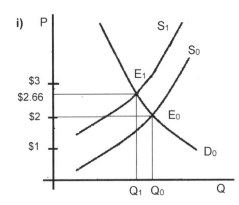

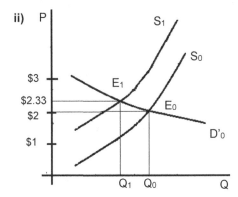

Image i: Consumer share of the total tax is $0.66 and supplier share is $0.34
Image ii: Consumer share of the total tax is $0.33 and supplier share is $0.67

- It is to be noted that if this tax is removed, new lower market equilibrium price will not reflect the exact tax difference either. It will shift supply curve to the right (resulting in increase in supply) and demand will increase.

Elasticity of Demand

- Elasticity of demand is the percentage change in quantities demanded divided by the percentage change in price.

$$E = \frac{(\%\ change\ in\ Quantity)}{(\%\ change\ in\ Price)} = \frac{\%\Delta Q}{\%\Delta P}$$

Classification of Elasticity of Demand

- Inelastic if $|E| < 1$
  It means % change in quantity < % change in price

- Elastic if $|E| > 1$
  It means % change in quantity > % change in price

- Unit Elastic if $|E| = 1$
  It means % change in quantity = % change in price

- Price elasticity of demand for goods with close substitute is higher than price elasticity of demands for goods with no close substitutes.

- In the following example, same change in price ΔP results in a different change in quantities demanded. Demand in image ii is relatively elastic as compared to the demand in image i

- Incidence of taxation is higher for consumers for the product with inelastic demand. It means that their share of tax is greater when demand is relatively inelastic.

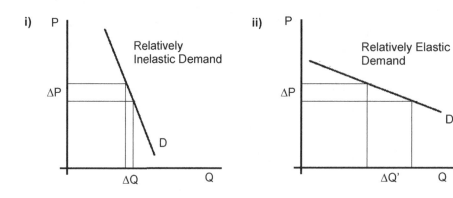

Elasticity Along a Linear Demand

- Elasticity of demand can be written as a product of two ratios:

$$E = \frac{\%\Delta Q}{\%\Delta P} = \frac{\Delta Q/Q}{\Delta P/P} = \frac{\Delta Q}{\Delta P} \times \frac{P}{Q}$$

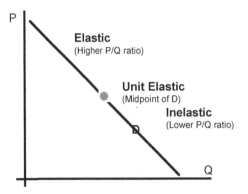

- If demand is a linear function it means that the first term, $\Delta Q/\Delta P$ (in above equation) is inverse of slope and remains constant. However, second ratio P/Q changes all along the curve.

- Since ratio, P/Q at the upper half is higher (higher value of P as compared to Q), demand curve is elastic. At lower half, due to lower P/Q ratio, it becomes inelastic. At midpoint, it is unit elastic.

- Therefore, every point on a linear demand curve (which is not horizontal or vertical) has a different elasticity.

Perfectly Elastic & Inelastic Cases

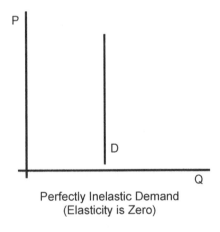

Perfectly Inelastic Demand
(Elasticity is Zero)

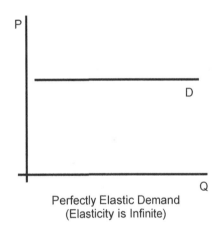

Perfectly Elastic Demand
(Elasticity is Infinite)

Midpoint Method for Elasticity

- Percentage changes are not symmetric i.e. percentage change between any two values depends on which value is chosen as the starting value and which one as the ending value.

  For example, if quantity demanded increases from 10 units to 15 units, percentage change is 50%, but in reverse (if it decreases from 15 to 10) reduction is not 50% but 33.3%.

  As a result, elasticity (calculated this way) is not a constant between two given points and its value depends on whether the price is increasing or decreasing.

- Value of elasticity between two points, obtained by using midpoint method, always has the same value whether the price increases or decreases:

$$E = \frac{\%\Delta Q}{\%\Delta P} = \frac{(\Delta Q / Q_{avg})}{(\Delta P / P_{avg})}$$

where:

$$Q_{avg} = (Q1 + Q2)/2$$
$$P_{avg} = (P1 + P2)/2$$

Elasticity of Supply

- Elasticity of supply is the percentage change in quantities supplied divided by the percentage change in price.

$$E = \frac{\%\ change\ in\ Quantity}{\%\ change\ in\ Price} = \frac{\%\Delta Q}{\%\Delta P}$$

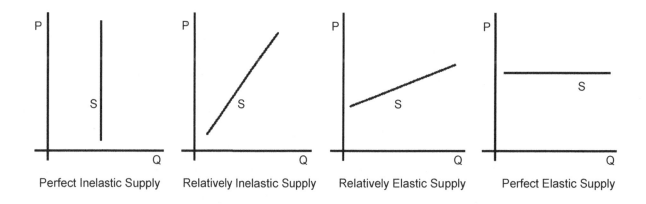

| Perfect Inelastic Supply | Relatively Inelastic Supply | Relatively Elastic Supply | Perfect Elastic Supply |

Consumer, Producer & Social Surplus

- *Consumer surplus* is the amount that individuals are willing to pay minus the amount that they actually pay for a service or a product.

    It is an area shown under the demand curve and above the price line.

    When the demand of a product or service is perfectly elastic, consumer surplus is zero because the price people pay equals to what they are willing to pay.

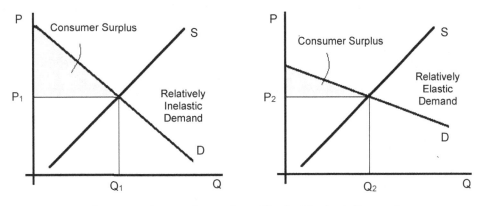

Consumer Surplus Comparison: Elastic & Inelastic Demand

- Consumer surplus increases as the product becomes inelastic. It becomes infinite for perfectly inelastic demand.

- **Producer surplus** is the amount producer of a good or a service receives and the minimum amount that producer is willing to accept.

  It is the area below market price and above supply curve

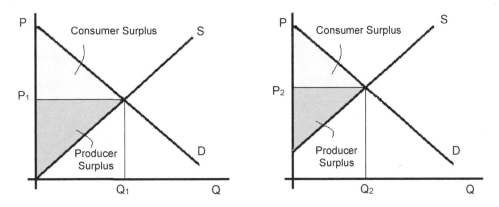

Impact of Supply Curve Shift on Consumer & Producer Surplus

Allocative Efficiency

- Social or economic surplus is the sum of consumer and producer surplus. Social surplus is largest at equilibrium point than it would be at any other price and quantity. This demonstrates that allocative efficiency is highest at market equilibrium.

  Allocative efficiency is therefore achieved with optimal distribution of goods or services while taking into account consumer's preferences.

- Allocative and productive efficiency (next chapter) are subsets of economic efficiency.

Chapter 03: Production, Cost & Revenue

Firms

- Firms hire or buy inputs in resource markets and produce outputs. Firms can be:

  Sole Proprietorship: Single owner who is responsible for all profits and losses.

  Partnership: Two or more joint owners who share profits & losses.

  Corporations: Independent entities with a legal identity separate from its owners. These are incorporated and the owners are called shareholders.

	Sole Proprietorships	Partnerships	Corporations
Number (millions)	23.4	3.3	5.8
Revenue (Trillions $)	1.26	4.45	25.12
Liability	Full	Full	Limited Liability

Owners in sole proprietorships and partnerships are fully liable. It means they are personally liable and responsible for payments if a firm incurs debt. (2012 US Stats)

Revenue, Cost & Profit

- Total Revenue is the unit price of a product multiplied by quantities sold.

- *Explicit Cost*: This is the cost that requires direct monetary payment e.g. wages, rent or other operating expenses etc.

- *Implicit Cost*: It is the opportunity cost of using resources. No actual payment is made for implicit cost.

- **Accounting Profit**
$$\Pi_{accy} = Total\ Revenue\ (TR) - Total\ Explicit\ Costs$$

- **Economic Profit**
$$\Pi = Total\ Revenue\ (TR) - Total\ Explicit\ Costs - Opportunity\ Costs$$

- A business may be generating positive accounting profit but economic profit can still be negative e.g. consider a scenario in which a shop owner is earning $1000 accounting profit, however he also has the option to rent the shop for $1500 (which is the opportunity cost). Therefore, economic profit (loss) in this case is going to be -$500.

Production Function

- A firm's output can be represented as a production function. It gives the quantities of output that can be produced using a certain combination of inputs. A simplified version can be expressed as:

$$Q = f(X_1, X_2, X_3, \ldots \ldots \ldots X_n)$$

Q is the output whereas $X_1, X_2, X_3, \ldots \ldots \ldots X_n$ are the quantities of factor inputs.

- Factor or resource inputs can be fixed or variable. For example, buildings and machineries are examples of capital and are considered fixed resources. Labor is considered a flexible resource and a variable input.

Short & Long Run

- **Short Run**: A firm is said to be in short run when it can change its output by changing any of its variable factor (such as labor, materials) but not by changing its fixed factors (such as plant capacity, building).

  Therefore, short run decisions involve a time horizon over which at least one of the inputs cannot be changed. These decisions are relatively easier to implement.

- **Long run**: A firm enters long run when it can change its scale of operations i.e. no factor of production is fixed, and all are variable.

  Long run decisions involve a time horizon over which firm can vary all of its inputs. These decisions are relatively difficult to implement.

  ### Short run, Long run & Market

- Short run and long run can be defined in terms of market dynamics as well.

- In short run the number of firms in an industry is fixed. However, a firm can always stop production (shut down) in short run. When a firm shuts down, it still incurs fixed cost and cannot exit the industry.

  In long run number of firms in an industry is not fixed. New firms are created and existing firms can exit the industry.

Marginal Product & Law of Diminishing Returns

- Total product is the output produced by using all inputs. Marginal product is the additional output that is generated when additional unit of a particular input is added assuming that other inputs are kept constant.

$$Marginal\ Product\ = \Delta Q / \Delta X$$

ΔQ is the change in quantity of output and ΔX is the change in quantity of input.

Law of Diminishing Returns

- The law states: "In a production process if one input is increased while all others are kept constant there is a point at which marginal per unit output will start to decrease". It is also known as the "law of diminishing marginal returns".

  e.g. if a company increases its labor but manufacturing capacity is kept constant, initially production will increase but there will be a point when adding labor will not yield additional output and it will eventually start to decline.

- Diminishing returns occur in short run.

- In the "most productive" region, output increases at an increasing rate, in the "diminishing return" region, it increases at a decreasing rate and then starts decreasing after point of maximum yield which is the region of "negative returns".

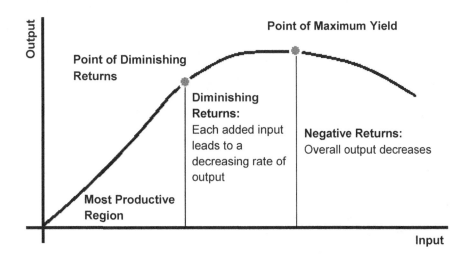

Total Cost, Average Total Cost & Marginal Cost

- A firm incurs fixed and variable costs in short run.

- **Fixed Cost:** Cost that firm must pay even when it doesn't produce anything. A firm cannot avoid fixed cost in short run. Rent is an example of a fixed cost.

- **Variable Cost:** It is associated with variable input and changes with the change in production quantity. It initially increases at an increasing rate with respect to the output, then at a decreasing rate before increasing at an increasing rate again.

Total Cost = Total Fixed Cost + Total Variable Cost

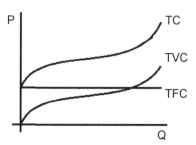

$$TC = TFC + TVC$$

- Labor is considered a variable cost.

- Total Cost includes opportunity cost as part of fixed or variable cost.

Average Total Cost

- Average total cost of producing quantity q is given as:

$$ATC = TC/q = (TFC + TVC)/q = AFC + AVC$$

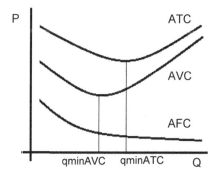

- Since TFC remains constant, AFC reduces with the increase in production quantity. It means ATC and AVC converge as production quantity, q increases.

- Production quantity at the minimum of AVC is always less than or equal to the quantity at minimum of ATC:

$$q_{min}AVC \leq q_{min}ATC$$

Marginal Cost

- Marginal cost (MC) can be defined as the cost of producing one extra unit of output. It is the change in total cost for any change in output.

$$MC = \frac{Change\ in\ TC}{Change\ in\ q} = \frac{\Delta TC}{\Delta q} = \frac{dTC}{dq} = Slope\ of\ TC$$

- Marginal cost is the slope of total cost curve. *TFC* (total fixed cost) has zero slope as it is constant and has no rate of change. Therefore, *MC* is also the slope of *TVC* (total variable cost) and is unaffected by changes in fixed costs.

$$TC \ = \ TVC \ + \ TFC$$

$$MC = \frac{dTC}{dq} = \ \frac{d(TFC)}{dq} + \frac{d(TVC)}{dq} \ = \ \frac{d(TVC)}{dq}$$

Marginal Product (MP) & Marginal Cost (MC)

- There is a reverse relationship between *MP* and *MC*. It means that as output decreases, marginal cost increases. When *MP* is at its peak, *MC* is at its minimum.

Input (Labor Quantity)	Total Cost	Output (Total Product)	Marginal Product	Marginal Cost
0	0	0	-	-
1	20	4	4	$5
2	40	9	5	$4
3	60	19	10	$2
4	80	39	20	$1
5	100	41	2	$10

Assuming each additional labor quantity adds $20 in cost

Marginal Cost & Cost Curves

- Marginal cost *(MC)* and average total cost *(ATC)* are connected. Marginal cost always crosses average total cost from below, at its minimum value.

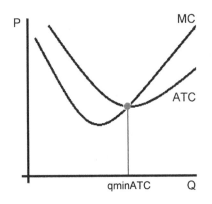 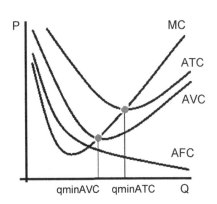

- When marginal cost is below average total cost, average total cost keeps falling, and when marginal cost is above average total cost, average total cost keeps rising.

- Just like *MC* curve crosses *ATC*, it also crosses *AVC* from below, and at its minimum value.

- MC curve has no relation with AFC curve.

Productive Efficiency

- A firm is most productively efficient at the minimum average total cost, which is also where **ATC = MC**.

  A firm can be productively efficient but have poor allocative efficiency. This is because allocative efficiency is achieved when social surplus is maximized with no deadweight loss.

Impact of Changing Costs on Cost Curves

- **Increase (decrease) in the cost of fixed input** results in *ATC* moving up (down). *MC* and *AVC* curves retain their positions and *MC* continues to intersect new *ATC'* at its minimum.

- **Increase (decrease) in the cost of variable input** results in *AVC*, *ATC* and *MC* moving up (down) as shown by *AVC'*, *ATC'* and *MC'*. The curves retain their shapes and relative orientations.

- **Improvement in technology** shifts one or both cost curves (fixed & variable) down depending on the nature of the change. MC continues to intersect *ATC* and *AVC* at their minimums. The difference between *ATC* and *AVC* is still *AFC* (average fixed cost).

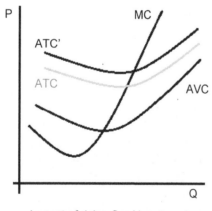

Impact of rising fixed input cost

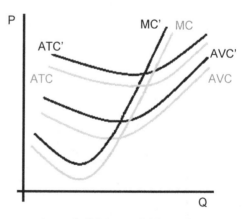

Impact of rising variable cost

Economies of Scale

- The concept of economies of scale is applicable to long run. It is the cost advantage that a firm obtains by changing its scale of production.

- Each firm has a short run average cost curve based on its own fixed and variable costs. In long run when a firm can vary all inputs and can change scale of production, it can move to a new short run average cost curve.

- If increasing scale of production results in a lower average cost curve, the firm experiences economies of scale. Diseconomies of scale results when firms become too large and average cost increases.

- Production is most efficient when ATC is at its minimum. Minimum efficient scale (*MES*) of production is the size of the firm when it can achieve minimum average cost in long run.

- Following graph shows three short term average cost curves (ATC_1, ATC_2, ATC_3) and a resulting **_long run average cost curve_** (*LRAC*)

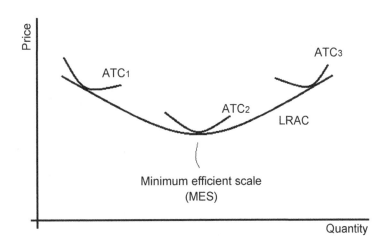

- Difference between short run average cost curve and economies of scale curve is that short run average cost curve assumes fixed costs and variable costs, whereas economies of scale curve is a long run average cost curve and all factors of production can change.

- Walmart is an example of a firm benefiting from economies of scale. Its size makes its processes more efficient and keeps costs low.

Chapter 04: Individual Firm Decisions

Profit Maximization

- Let's assume following two conditions for a firm that wants to maximize profit:
    - It knows its own cost curves
    - Exogenous market price, p_0 of its product that it cannot change

- Economic profit: $\Pi = TR - TC$

    TC is total cost including opportunity cost
    TR is total revenue. For quantity, q it is equal to:

    $$TR = p_o . q$$

- **Marginal Revenue**, MR is additional revenue generated by selling additional unit of product i.e. it is slope of TR:

    $$MR = \frac{d(TR)}{dq}$$

    For fixed price, MR is always going to be constant and equal to p_0

- Marginal Cost, MC is slope of TC

    $$MC = \frac{d(TC)}{dq}$$

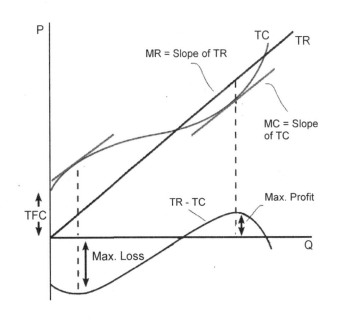

- Maximum gap between TC & TR represents maximum profit as well as maximum loss. Such gap exists between two functions at a point when slopes of both functions become equal.

    $$\frac{d(TR)}{dq} = \frac{d(TC)}{dq}$$

    $$MC = MR$$

- Therefore, Maximum economic profit, $\Pi_{max} = Max\ (TR - TC)$ exists when $MC = MR$. Maximum loss can be found in a similar way as it is also $Max\ (TR - TC)$.

In the following example, output quantity, total cost and product price are assumed, whereas the other quantities have been calculated:

Output Quantity	TC ($)	MC ($)	Price ($) (per unit)	TR ($)	MR ($)	Profit ($)
10	110	11	10	100	10	-10
20	200	9	10	200	10	0
30	260	6	10	300	10	40
40	310	5	10	400	10	110
50	340	3	10	500	10	160
60	400	6	10	600	10	200
70	490	9	10	700	10	210
80	610	12	10	800	10	190
90	740	13	10	900	10	170

- If, in this example, firm can only produce the product in multiples of 10, it needs to produce 70 units to maximize profit at $MR \cong MC$.

Marginal Revenue, Marginal Cost & Exogenous Price

- We know:

  MR is constant and equal to p_0 .

  Maximum profit exists when $MC = MR$

  Total Revenue, $TR = q_0 \cdot p_0$

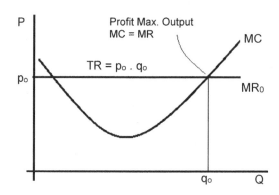

- $TC = ATC \times q_0$

- Total profit can be calculated.
  $$\begin{aligned} \Pi &= TR - TC \\ &= (q_0 \times p_0) - (ATC \times q_0) \\ &= q_0 (p_0 - ATC) \\ &= q_0 (MR - ATC) \end{aligned}$$

  This means that profit can be calculated by using values of ATC, MC and MR at q_0.

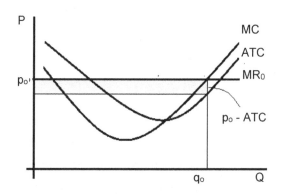

Impact of Cost & Revenue on Profit

- In presence of exogenous price p_0, a change in total fixed cost *(TFC),* shifts *TC* curve; *MC* remains unimpacted.
It does not impact *TR* curve either, therefore *MR* remains same as well.
Economic profit i.e. *Max (TR - TC)* increases or decreases depending on whether fixed cost decreases or increases.

- In presence of exogenous price p_0, a change in *TVC,* changes both *TC* curve and *MC curve.*
TR curve and MR curve remain unchanged.
Economic profit i.e. *Max (TR - TC)* changes depending on the change in *TC* curve.

- A decrease or increase in only exogenous price p_0 makes *TR* curve less or more steep. MR curve changes (moves up or down) as well.
TC curve and *MC* remain same.
Economic profit increases or decreases depending on whether the new price is more or less as compared to the original price.

Negative Profit (Loss) & Its Impact

- If *ATC* is above *MR* at all points (exogenous price p_0), it means firm is generating negative profit (losses). *TC* in this case is always going to be higher than *TR.*

- In long run (where no factor of production is fixed), if economic profit goes in negative, it means firm can exit the industry.

- In short run (where a firm cannot avoid or change its fixed cost), if economic profit goes into negative the firm needs to decide:

    o Whether to continue producing at *MR = MC* until it can exit in long run **OR**
    o Shutdown i.e. stop production until exit.

- Decision to continue or stop production can be made using following condition:

    o If *TR < TVC* of a product at *MR = MC*
    Then Stop Production

When *TR < TVC*, it means that loss is occurring not only because of fixed cost but variable cost (due to production) is resulting into additional losses.

Example

- Consider a case (image i) where *AVC > MR* at all points. It means that firm's total revenue *(TR)* is less than its total variable cost *(TVC)*.

  ○ $Total\ Revenue = Area\ (Z)$
  ○ $Total\ Cost = Area\ (X + Y + Z)$
  ○ $Total\ Variable\ Cost = Area\ (Y + Z)$
  ○ $Total\ Fixed\ Cost = Area\ (X)$
  ○ $Economic\ Losses\ =\ Area\ (X + Y)$

- Total cost is sum of *TVC* and *TFC*. *TR* less than *TVC* implies that firm is incurring extra losses due to production.
- It is better to shut down production in short run as losses will be reduced to area "X".

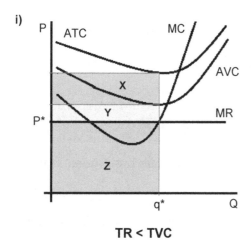
TR < TVC

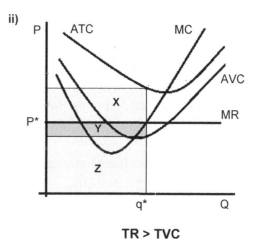
TR > TVC

- When *AVC < MR* (at *MR = MC*) as shown in image (ii), it means *TR* is greater than *TVC* which can help offset fixed cost losses.

- In example:
  ○ $Total\ Revenue = Area\ (Y + Z)$
  ○ $Total\ Cost = Area\ (X + Y + Z)$
  ○ $Total\ Variable\ Cost = Area\ (Z)$
  ○ $Total\ Fixed\ Cost = Area\ (X + Y)$
  ○ $Economic\ Losses = Area\ (X)$

Here *TR > TVC* by area "Y"; this amount is going to cover some proportion of *TFC*. Therefore, the firm should keep producing until it enters long run.

Chapter 05: Perfect Competition

Market Comparison & Perfect Competition

- Competitiveness of industries in a market varies between two extremes i.e. from monopoly (1 firm) to perfect competition (large number of firms).

Market Power →

	Perfect Competition	*Monopolistic Competition*	*Oligopoly*	*Monopoly*
Number of Firms	Large	Many	Few	One
Product Type	Identical	Differentiated	Identical/ Differentiated	Unique
Ease of Entry	High	High	Low	Blocked
Price	Equal to MC	Greater than MC	Greater than MC	Greater than MC
SR Profit	+ve, -ve, zero	+ve, -ve, zero	+ve, -ve, zero	+ve, -ve, zero
LR Profit	Zero	Zero	+ve, zero	+ve, zero
Example	Agriculture products	Clothing, Restaurants	Automobiles, Computers	Power distribution

Perfect Competition

- For a market to be in perfect competition few conditions need to be fulfilled:
    - There is a large number of relatively small buyers and sellers
    - All firms produce identical or homogeneous products
    - There is a freedom of entry and exit
    - There is perfect information and knowledge

- These conditions imply that all firms are **price takers** which means that they cannot influence market price of the product, therefore all firm's demand curves are perfectly elastic.

- Example of Perfect Competition:
    - Foreign exchange market
    - Agricultural markets

- Firms in perfect competition maximize profit by producing output when *MC = MR*.

Supply Curve in a Perfectly Competitive Market

- If q_i is the individual firm output and Q is the total market output of that product.

$$Q = \sum_{i=1}^{N} q_i$$

- For an individual firm in a short run MC and AVC curves are shown.

- In a competitive market, all firms are price takers. Every additional product is sold for the same price which means MR (from every additional product) is same as the market price.

- If market price of product changes, MR changes as well.

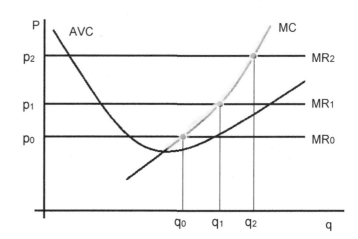

For a different market price, MR intersects MC curve at a different point. All highlighted points on MC curve (above AVC curve) are such points of intersections. Combination of these points is the supply curve of that firm.

Market Supply Curve

- Sum of all such supply curves of a product by different firms represents market supply curve.
- While market price is same for all firms, individual supply curves are different for different firms depending on their own fixed or variable costs etc.
- Market supply curve along with an individual firm supply curve is shown below.

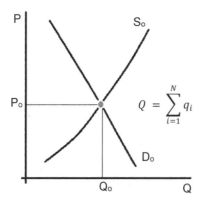

Market Supply Curve

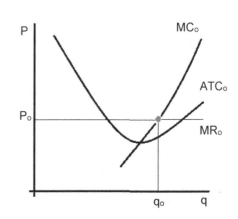

Individual Firm Supply Curve

Short-run Equilibrium

- Short-run equilibrium in a perfectly competitive market is achieved when:
  - Market is in equilibrium i.e. supply is equal to demand.
  - Sum of level of production of all firms is equal to the market demand.
  - Each firm's level of production maximizes its economic profit (*MR = MC for every firm*)

- In short run, increase in demand of a product (right shift of demand curve) results in increase in prices and output quantity. Similarly, decrease in demand results in decrease in prices and output.

- In short run, economic profits can be positive (supernormal), zero (normal) or negative.

Long-run Equilibrium

- When economic profits are made, new firms are attracted into the industry.
- This results in:
  - Increase in production which moves market supply curve to the right.
  - Market demand curve remains same, so the price goes down
  - Decrease in price reduces economic profit of all firms
  - As long as economic profits are positive, new firms keep adding production, shifting supply curve to the right. Economic profit of each firm keeps on reducing until it goes to zero.

- This results in a long-run equilibrium.

- Therefore, a long-run equilibrium is a market price such that:
  - At the market price, market quantity demanded equals market quantity supplied
  - Each firm's level of production maximizes the firm's economic profit
  - Each firm earns zero economic profit.

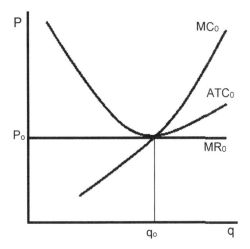

- This doesn't mean that firms are losing money. ***When economic profit is zero, accounting profit can still be positive***.

- In long run equilibrium, the incentive to enter or exit a market disappears.

- It is to be noted that long run equilibrium condition is achieved at the minimum efficient scale (*MES*) i.e. when the long run average cost curve is at the minimum. Firms and market cannot utilize resources for production more efficiently than at this point.

Economic Efficiency

- Perfectly competitive market achieves highest allocative efficiency in both short and long run as equilibrium prices are equal to *MC* and social surplus is maximum.

- Output in long run is produced at the minimum average total cost, *ATC*. This means perfect competition achieves highest productive efficiency in long run.

Change in Demand & Long-run Equilibrium

- In long-run, increase in demand in a perfectly competitive market causes:

  - Increase in prices, due to the right shift in demand curve.
  - Initially, with an increase in demand, firms start earning greater economic profits.
  - This attracts additional firms to enter the market, market supply increases and prices decrease towards previous levels.
  - If cost conditions remain unchanged, then prices revert to what they were before the increase in demand.

- In long-run, decrease in demand in a perfectly competitive market causes:

  - Decrease in prices, due to the left shift in demand curve.
  - Initially, with a decrease in demand, firms undergo economic losses.
  - Over time, these losses result in firms exiting the market, market supply decreases and prices start increasing towards previous levels.
  - If cost conditions remain unchanged, prices revert to what they were before the decrease in demand.

Chapter 06: Monopoly

- A pure monopoly is defined as a single seller of a product or service with no threat of entry.

- A firm may gain monopoly because of following reasons:
  - Being first in that field
  - Mergers
  - Higher efficiency
  - Control of resources
  - It is efficient to have a monopoly in a certain field.

- Monopoly maximizes profit where *MR = MC*.
- Monopoly results in price setting by the firm rather than price set by competition i.e. monopolist firm is **price maker** not taker.

Marginal Revenue

- Total Revenue is market price multiplied by quantity:
  $$TR = P \times Q$$

  A general equation of the demand curve graph with downward slope (-b) can be written as:

  $$P = a - bQ$$
  $$TR = (a - bQ) \times Q$$
  $$TR = aQ - bQ^2$$

  MR is change in total revenue per quantity.

  $$MR = \frac{d(TR)}{dQ}$$
  $$MR = a - 2bQ$$

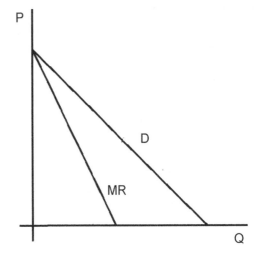

- This means slope of MR is twice much as that of slope of demand curve.

Profit Maximization

- Maximum profit occurs at *MR = MC*.
- Plotting *MC* on the graph, gives maximum profit price and corresponding quantity.
- Plotting *ATC* on graph gives amount of profit as well (shown by darker shaded area).

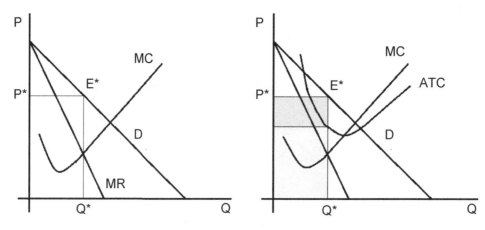

Firm produces Q* where MR=MC and charges price P* using demand curve

- In order to sell additional units, monopolist has to reduce the price for all quantities (every single unit). Therefore, not only marginal revenue from additional unit sold is lower, but revenue from previous units is reduced as well. This is known as price effect. There is no price effect for a competitive firm as it sells at a given price.

Monopoly & Deadweight Loss

- In case of a competitive market, market supply and demand is in equilibrium at price P' and quantity Q'.

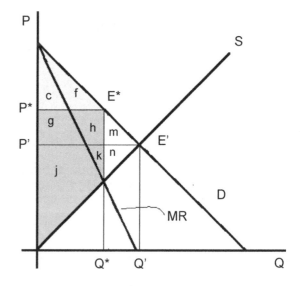

Monopoly Vs. Free Market

- Consumer surplus is:
  $$= Area\ (c + f + g + h + m)$$
  Producer surplus is:
  $$= Area\ (j + k + n)$$

- Once the market is monopolized, consumer surplus reduces to:
  $$= Area\ (c + f)$$

- Producer surplus increases:
  $$= Area\ (g + h + j + k)$$

- It also results in deadweight loss:
  $$= Area\ (m + n)$$

- While producer surplus increases, social surplus which is the sum of consumer and producer surplus decreases.

- Monopolist firm not only results in price increase as compared with perfect competition, product quantity is reduced as well.

Short run and Long run

- In short run if demand is not sufficient anymore (e.g. because of recession), economic profits may become negative. Therefore, profits in short run can be positive, negative or zero.

- In long run, the monopolist can change its scale of production to maximize profits. Since there is a barrier to entry, it is not necessary for the monopolist to achieve optimal scale (which is the minimum of long run average cost curve). Such decision is based entirely on market demand.

- The existence of barrier to entry prevents firms to enter the market in long run. It is therefore, possible for a firm to continue making positive economic profits in long run. Economic profits in the long run can be both positive or zero.

Economic Efficiency:

- Monopoly equilibrium does not achieve allocative efficiency in short or long run as prices are higher than *MC* and social surplus is not maximum.

- Because output quantities produced are less than the output quantities at minimum *ATC*; productive efficiency is not achieved either.

Natural Monopoly

- Natural monopoly occurs when the most efficient number of firms in the industry is one.
- A natural monopoly exists typically in situations when there is very high fixed cost associated with the product. This means that increase in production reduces average total cost.
- Natural monopolies need government regulation.

Example:

- Power lines & electricity distribution system is very expensive and impractical to be installed by multiple companies. It is therefore natural for a company to have a monopoly in distribution while multiple companies produce electricity.
- Other examples include water supply, gas supply, railway infrastructure etc.

Chapter 07: Monopolistic Competition

- Perfect competition and monopoly represent two extremes of market competition. Monopolistic market is an imperfectly competitive market that defines vast majority of real world firms.

- There are large number of firms in monopolistic market but their products are differentiated i.e. products differ slightly from competitive products; e.g. clothing, restaurants etc.

- Differentiated products may have different public perception because of different strategies including advertising, brand names or even location where the product is sold. This gives each firm some sort of monopoly. Unlike perfect competition, packaging, branding and marketing is very important in monopolistic competition.

- Firms maximize profit at $MC = MR$. Ease of entry in the market is high (better than oligopoly) but less than perfect competition.

- Firms are price makers not takers but price elasticity of demand is higher than in monopoly.

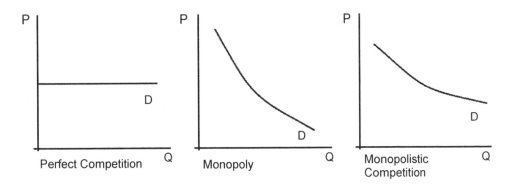

Short run Equilibrium

- Economic profits made by firms in monopolistic competition in short run can be of any level i.e. positive, zero or negative.

- An example of a firm making supernatural (positive) profit in short run is shown in the image.

- P_0 and q_0 is the price and quantity of a firm's product. C is the value of ATC at q_0. Profit is shown by the shaded area.

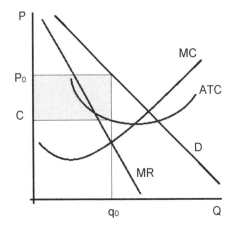

Long run Equilibrium

- Positive economic profits attract new firms to enter business in long run.

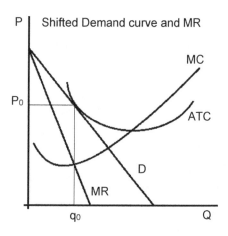

- As quantities of new products increase in the market, the demand of products of existing firms decreases. This results in a left shift of demand curve of individual firms. With the shift in demand curve, *MR* curve shifts left as well.

- New firms keep adding and demand curve continues shifting until it becomes tangent to the average cost curve. This means the economic profits are reduced to zero.

- It is possible that demand falls below long run average cost (LRAC). Firms will exit because of the negative economic profits. As a result, demand curve will shift right leading to a situation when losses reduce and profit becomes zero again.

  Therefore, in monopolistic competition firms earn normal (zero) economic profits.

Economic Efficiency

- Unlike perfect competition (and like monopoly), monopolist market does not achieve allocative efficiency in short or long run as equilibrium prices are higher than *MC*. However, the impact is less severe than monopoly.

- Monopolistic market does not achieve productive efficiency either. Firms produce product quantities which are less than the quantities at minimum *ATC*.

Chapter 08: Oligopoly & Game Theory

- It is an industry dominated by a few firms i.e. between monopoly and perfect competition.

- Key features are:
  - ○ ***Conjectural Interdependence***: It means that firms are affected by how other firms set prices and output.
  - ○ There are barriers to entry, but these are less than monopoly.
  - ○ Number of firms in oligopoly is less than monopolistic competition.
  - ○ Products can be identical or differentiated.

- Auto industry is an example of oligopoly.
- Duopoly is a form of oligopoly where only two firms exist in industry e.g. Marvel & DC comics.

- Because of conjectural interdependence, firms may not only seek to maximize profits but also market share which can result in competition, known as non-collusive oligopoly. Another possibility for firms in oligopoly is to **collude** to maximize profit.

Non-Collusive Oligopoly

- Consider a firm in a competitive oligopoly supplies Q_0 quantities at price P_0. If it increases its product price, competitors may not follow. As a result, firm with price increase may lose market share and observe a decrease in *TR*.

  It implies that firm, after increasing price, is going to experience relatively elastic demand.

- If a firm reduces its price, other firms will follow to maintain their market share. This means demand will be relatively inelastic for all firms. This will result in fall in revenue for everyone

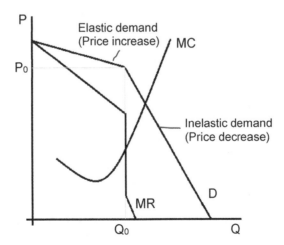

Individual Firm's **Kinked Demand Curve** in Non-Collusive Oligopoly

Collusive Oligopoly

- Due to conjectural interdependence, firms may form a cartel to collude on price and set profit maximizing levels of outputs.

- Cartel reduces total market quantity to fix higher prices. However, it sets the quantity such that the prices (P_{fix}) do not go higher than monopoly prices (P_m): $P_{fix} \leq P_m$

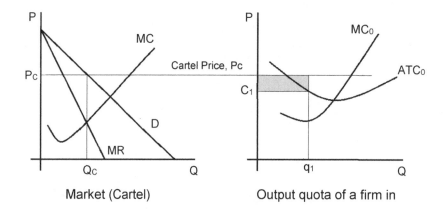

Market (Cartel)   Output quota of a firm in

- A **quota system** is needed to achieve high prices. Using quota, each firm's production is reduced such that their combined outputs is equal to the desired cartel market output.

- Individual firm output is not most efficient i.e. *MC* is not equal to *MR* at this new level of production. However, since firms are not price takers anymore, higher prices mean higher profits.

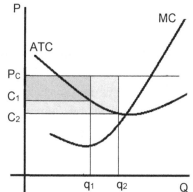

- Due to increased profit, it is more attractive for colluding firms to increase production secretly. As shown in the image firms can earn greater profit (lighter & darker shaded area) by producing quantities q_2 instead of q_1.

- It means that collusion needs some policing or **control mechanism**; otherwise excess production, can destabilize cartel.

- In US, Section 1 of Sherman antitrust act prohibits restraint of trade including price fixing. It also prohibits other aspects e.g. collusion to reduce spending in advertising.

Economic Efficiency

- In oligopoly, economic profits (like monopoly) can be positive, negative or zero in short run & positive or zero in long run. Just like monopoly or monopolistic market, oligopoly market does not achieve economic efficiency (productive or allocative).

Price Stability:

• In cartel, price stability is achieved through collusion and policing mechanism.

• Kinked demand curve in collusive oligopoly shows that decrease or increase in prices by a firm does not maximize profit. This explains why prices tend to remain stable in non-collusive oligopoly. However, it does not explain how the market price is set in market in first place.

• There are other explanations of price stability as well: Many firms set prices based on marginal cost, percentage of fixed cost and certain profit margin. They also consider industry averages to estimate a fair price. Prices remain stable as long as costs remain unchanged. This is known as *marginal cost plus pricing*.

  Sometimes a price leader exists in oligopoly e.g. it can be the largest firm in oligopoly. If such a firm keeps prices stable, other firms follow.

Herfindahl-Hirschman Index

• It is a measure of industry concentration and a method to summarize the degree to which oligopoly exists in the industry.

  HHI is calculated by squaring the market share of each firm:

$$HHI = (Market\ Share\ 1)^2 + (Market\ Share\ 2)^2 + \ldots\ldots + (Market\ Share\ n)^2$$

HHI Index	Concentration Ratio
0 – 1500	Low
1500 – 2500	Moderate
2500 – 10,000	High

• A high *HHI* index number indicates a high degree of concentration. *It* increases as the market share of a firm increases. A monopolist firm has an HHI of 10,000 (100^2).

  In a perfectly competitive market, due to low market share of each firm, *HHI* approaches zero, e.g. *HHI* of 50 firms, with market share of 0.1% each, would be 0.5.

• *Example: HHI* of four firms with market share of 40%, 30%, 20% and 10% would be:

$$HHI = (40)^2 + (30)^2 + (20)^2 + (10)^2 = 3000$$

• If in a highly-concentrated market *HHI* increases by more than 200 points due to a merger, it raises antitrust concerns. It should also be noted that number of firms do not necessarily give indication about market concentration as it depends on the share of each firm.

Game Theory

- Due to mutual interdependence of firms which increases complexity of oligopoly, there is no single theory on how oligopolies behave.

- Economists use game theory to analyze such situations. It helps in explaining how players make decisions and receive payoffs based on other player's decisions.

- Kinked demand curve discussed earlier is a limited form of game theory.

Cooperative & Noncooperative Games

- A game is *cooperative* if players can sign binding contracts that are enforced through some mechanism.

  A game is *noncooperative* if players cannot sign contracts or if agreements are to be self-enforced.

- Non-cooperative games can be extensive form games or normal form games.

- *Extensive form games* are also known as *sequential games*.

  In such games, later players have some knowledge about earlier actions. It does not need to be a perfect information. These games are usually represented in the form of decision trees.

- *Normal form games* are also known as *simultaneous games*.

  In such games both players move (or do not move) simultaneously without any information about the action of the other player. These games are usually represented by payoff matrices.

Prisoner's Dilemma

- It is a scenario in which two people might not cooperate even if it appears that that gains from cooperation are larger.
- This is an example of simultaneous games and applies to oligopoly as well.

- Two prisoner's A and B are in separate rooms without any mode of communication with each other.

  Prosecutors lack evidence, but encourage each prisoner to confess by informing that the other has already signed a confession. The offer is:

- o If both A & B confess they each get 3 years in prison.
- o If either one confesses but the other does not; the one who confesses gets away free and the other gets 6 years in prison.
- o However, if no-one confesses, both get 1 year in prison.

		B	
		No Confession	**Confession**
A	**No Confession**	A: 1yr, B: 1yr	A: 6yrs, B: Free
	Confession	A: Free, B: 6yrs	A: 3yrs, B: 3yrs

- The key in this scenario is that both A and B have incentive to confess regardless of what choice the other makes. This is explained as below:

  If B does not confess, A should defect (confess) because A will be set free.
  If B confesses, A should confess too, otherwise A will get larger sentence.

  This means that regardless of what action B takes, A should always defect (confess). Similar analysis applies to B as well.

- The dilemma is that even though staying silent (cooperation) offers better reward; it is not the rational outcome from a self-interested perspective.

Strictly Dominant Strategy & Equilibrium

- In above example because confession is always a better payoff, regardless of the other player's choice, confession is a *strictly dominant strategy* for both A and B.

  An equilibrium in dominant strategies exists if all players have a dominant strategy.

- "No confession", in this example, is therefore a "**strictly *dominated strategy***". A rational player will never play a dominated strategy.

Weakly Dominant Strategy

- A strategy is **weakly dominant strategy** for a player, if no matter what the other players does, the strategy is at least as good as the other strategy and in some situation better than the other strategy. A rational player with weakly dominant strategy will play that strategy.

- Any strictly dominant strategy is also a weakly dominant strategy. In above example, confession is a weakly dominant strategy also, as it offers at least as good or better position than the other strategy.

- Consider another example in which the prisoners have following options:

		B	
		No Confession	Confession
A	No Confession	A: 1yr, B: 1yr	A: 6yrs, B: 1yr
	Confession	A: 1yr, B: 6yrs	A: 5yrs, B: 5yrs

- Prisoner A: If B doesn't confess, it doesn't matter which strategy A chooses
                  If B confesses, A should confess too to get less prison time

  Prisoner B: If A doesn't confess, it doesn't matter which strategy B chooses
                  If A confesses, B should confess too to get less prison time.

- Therefore, confession is a weakly dominant strategy for both A & B. Confession by both is weakly dominant strategy equilibrium.

Nash Equilibrium

- Nash equilibrium is a solution concept of non-cooperative games involving two or more players in which each player is assumed to know the equilibrium strategies of the other players, and no player has anything to gain by changing only his or her own strategy.

  It offers a stable situation that no player wants to deviate from.

- In the first example of prisoner's dilemma, mutual defection is the only Nash Equilibrium since each player could only do worse by unilaterally changing strategy.

- Any dominant strategy equilibrium is always a Nash Equilibrium, however not every Nash Equilibrium is a dominant strategy equilibrium.

  ### Examples:

		Player 1	
		Y	Z
Player 2	A	Player2: 0, Player1: 0	Player2: 1, Player1: 1
	B	Player2: 1, Player1: 1	Player2: 1, Player1: 1

- No player has strictly dominant strategy.

- Player 1 has weakly dominant strategy, Z & player A has weakly dominant strategy, B.

- (Z, B) is a Nash equilibrium. None of the player gains anything by independently changing his strategy.

  (A, Z) & (B, Y) are also Nash equilibriums. This is because from either of these strategies, none of the player gains anything by changing his own strategy.

- Consider another example where competing Store A and B have following gains by providing high or low discounts to customers in their stores

	Profit (m)	Store B	
		No Discount	**Discount**
Store A	**No Discount**	Store A: 15, Store B: 15	Store A: 10, Store B: 20
	Discount	Store A: 20, Store B: 10	Store A: 12, Store B: 12

- In this example giving discounts is the strictly dominant strategy of both stores. This is the only Nash equilibrium as well.

- Firms in oligopoly face these dilemmas as well.

- It is to be noted that if, in the previous example, both firms can collude, each can earn greater profits by not offering discounts to customers.

  Easiest approach in this case for oligopoly firms would be to sign a contract. This is illegal in US.

- OPEC (Organization of Petroleum Exporting Countries), which is not bound by any laws, has signed international agreements to act like a monopoly and hold down petroleum output to keep prices higher and make high profits.

Chapter 09: Price Strategy

- Firms try to maximize profitability for every unit sold by employing different strategies.

  Price discrimination is one such price strategy in which different prices to different consumers are charged for the same good or service, for reasons not associated with the cost of supply.

Conditions for Price Discrimination

- Firms must have sufficient monopoly i.e. they are not price takers.
- Different market segments must be identified i.e. consumers with different price elasticity of demand.
- There is sufficient information and ability to separate different groups.
- There must be ability to prevent arbitrage i.e. consumers cannot purchase at the lower price and then resell it. This is easier to achieve for services than goods.

- There are three types of price discrimination: First Degree, Second Degree, Third Degree.

First Degree Price Discrimination

- It is also known as perfect price discrimination.
- Unlike monopoly, where the seller charges one fixed price to everyone, in first degree price discrimination, the monopoly seller charges a maximum price that every consumer is willing to pay, therefore, there is no fixed price.
- Since every additional product is sold at the maximum price, MR shifts to the demand curve and consumer surplus reduces to zero.

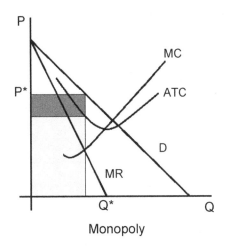

Monopoly

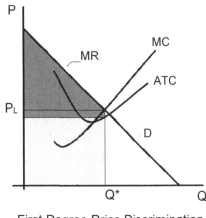

First Degree Price Discrimination

- Minimum price of the product charged by the firm is going to be equal to the marginal cost of the product.

- Darker shaded area of the graph shows how this strategy maximizes profit.

- This kind of price discrimination is not easy to achieve as it is very difficult for any firm to figure out the price each consumer is willing to pay.

Second Degree Price Discrimination

- Second degree price discrimination involves charging different pricing for different quantities. It is achieved by offering larger quantities at lower prices. Such nonlinear pricing helps producers in capturing large portion of total market surplus.

- Example shows three levels of pricing. Consumers are offered quantities Q_1, Q_2 and Q_3 for P_1, P_2 and P_3 respectively.

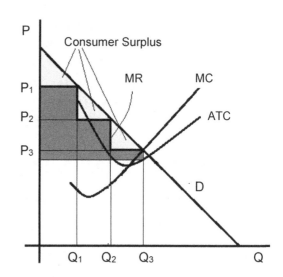

- MR is a step function because fixed price is charged for a defined number of quantities. Therefore, for same number of quantities, revenue generated from additional output is constant.

- Profit is shown by the darker areas, where as lighter areas represent consumer surplus. This way more profit can be achieve than monopoly.

Third Degree Price Discrimination

- Third degree price discrimination occurs when a seller identifies two (or more) separate groups of buyers that have different demand elasticities.
- In such case sellers raise profits by setting different prices for the separate groups. Firms charge higher to the consumers with inelastic demand whereas they charge lower to the consumers with elastic demand.
- Example of this is cinema tickets, where the students or seniors ticket pricing is lower due to their relatively elastic demand.

No Price Discrimination

- Image (i) and (ii) shows demand curves of a same product of two groups.

- 1st image shows inelastic demand (D_1 with marginal revenue, MR_1) whereas second graph shows elastic demand (D_2 with marginal revenue, MR_2). Image (iii) shows combined D^* and MR^* of both groups.

- If there is no price discrimination, price will be same for both consumer groups. Using the combined graph, producer will find the price P^* where $MC = MR^*$.
  This price is then used to find the total Quantities (Q_1 and Q_2) for both demand curves.

- In such case:
  - MC is equal to the combined Marginal Revenue, MR^*
  - Price P^* is same for both consumer groups.
  - $Q_1 + Q_2 = Q^*$
  - Profit can be found using ATC curve (C is the value ATC for quantity Q^*). Total profit is equal to the profit from each individual group.

- Using this strategy $MC = MR^*$ but $MR_1 < MR^*$ and $MR_2 > MR^*$. This means the firm can transfer some products from 1st consumer group to the 2nd to increase profit.
  This is achieved through price discrimination.

No Price Discrimination

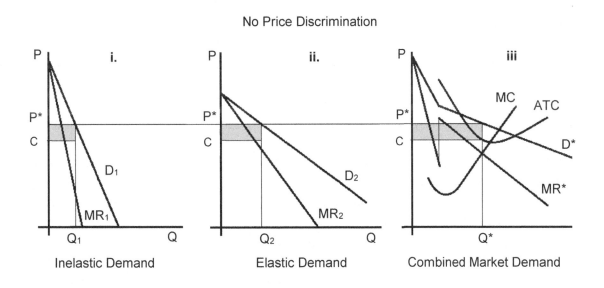

| Inelastic Demand | Elastic Demand | Combined Market Demand |

Price Discrimination

- In order to maximize profit, firm initially finds the value of marginal revenue (where $MC = MR^*$) from the combined demand curves MR^* and D^* (image iii).
  It then uses this MC value to find price P_1, Q_1' for 1st market and P_2, Q_2' for 2nd market.

- In such case
  - $MR_1 = MR_2 = MR^* = MC$
  - Higher price P_1 is charged to the consumers with inelastic demand curve, whereas relatively lower price P_2 is charged to the consumer with elastic demand curve.
  - While the total quantities sold is still the same as in previous case, the quantities in individual markets have been redistributed to maximize profit.
  - $Q_1' + Q_2' = Q^*$

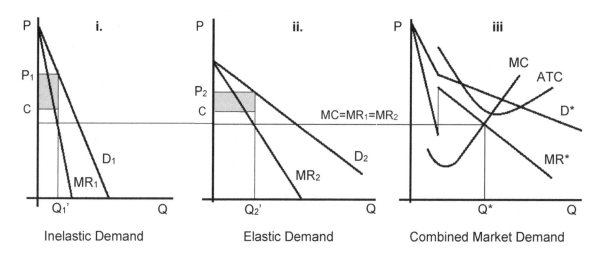

Price Discrimination

| i. | ii. | iii |
| Inelastic Demand | Elastic Demand | Combined Market Demand |

Other Price Strategies

- **Price skimming** strategy means that firms set higher rates during introductory phase of a product or service. It allows them to maximize profits and also cover cost of investment that has gone in the research for the product.
  This strategy targets early adopters of a product who have relatively inelastic demand.

- **Economy pricing** strategy involves minimizing marketing and production costs to attract most price-conscious consumers.
  Generic food suppliers and discount retailers like Walmart use this strategy. Profitability is based on sales volume; therefore, this strategy is difficult for small retailers to adopt.

- **Premium pricing** means buyers have tendency to assume that expensive items are more desirable and offer better quality. Businesses create a value perception by charging higher prices for their products that are not necessarily of better quality.
  Such pricing strategy needs better marketing, packaging etc.

- **Psychology pricing** is a way to enhance value of a product by pricing it in such a way e.g. a price of $9.99 appears better than $10.00 and creates an illusion of enhanced value.

- **Bundle pricing** means selling multiple products for a price lower than the sum of individual price of the products. This creates a value perception.

Chapter 10: Market Failure

Market Failure

- It is a situation in which allocation of goods or services is not efficient. Market failure exists when individual interest leads to net social welfare loss.

- It can occur because of:
  - Monopoly Privileges
  - Asymmetric Information
  - Externalities etc.

Asymmetric Information

- When one party knows more than the other during a transaction it is known as asymmetric information.

Adverse Selection

- Adverse selection occurs when there's a lack of symmetric information prior to a deal between buyer and seller.

  Example: A person buying health insurance may hide the fact that he smokes, thereby paying as much premium as by a non-smoker. This is a disadvantage for the insurance company.

Moral Hazard

- Moral hazard is the risk that someone takes because someone else bears the cost of those risks.
- It occurs when there is:
  i.   Asymmetric information between the parties and
  ii. Change in behavior of one party after a deal is struck.

  Example: A person may start driving less carefully after getting insurance and become a bigger accident risk.

Externalities

- Externalities are costs or benefits arising from an economic activity that affect people other than those engaged in the activity. These are spill-over effects arising from either production or consumption of a product or service.
- Externality can be: Positive or Negative

Negative Externality

- Negative externality occurs when an individual or firm making a decision does not have to pay the full cost of the decision.

- If a product has a negative externality, then the cost to society is greater than the cost consumer is paying. It results in market inefficiencies unless proper action is taken.

Example

- Obesity from fast food consumption or methane emissions from cattle are negative externalities.
  Water pollution caused by different industries reduces fish supply. This will result in economic losses for the fishermen.

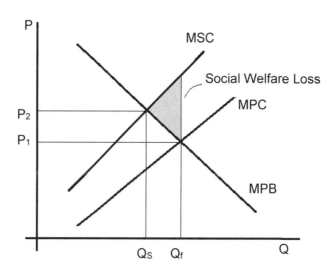

- Q_f is free market quantity, Q_s is social optimum quantity. $Q_f > Q_s$

- MPB is *Marginal Private Benefit*. If consumers are the only group deriving benefit from a product or service, then the demand curve is the marginal social benefit curve.

- MPC is *Marginal Private Cost* and is equivalent to Marginal Cost.

- MSC is *Marginal Social Cost*. It is the cost society pays to produce an additional unit.

- *Social Welfare Loss* is a deadweight loss. It is a cost to society due to market inefficiency.

- There are different ways to deal with negative externalities and reduce social welfare loss. This includes limited permits, caps (putting limits), taxation or even direct control by the government.

Positive Externality

- A positive externality is a benefit that is enjoyed by a third-party because of an economic transaction.

- Education is a positive externality. Besides helping the students directly, it also helps society in the form of more economic activity & lower crime rates etc.
Another example is the landscape improvement of a neighborhood which increases property prices of all home owners.

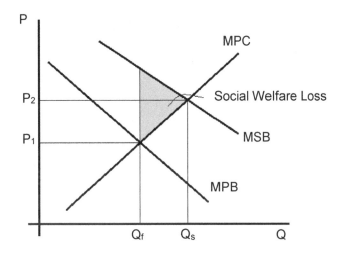

- Q_f is free market quantity whereas Q_s is optimal social output. In presence of positive externality $Q_s > Q_f$

- MPB is marginal private benefit.

- MSB is **Marginal Social Benefit**. It is the total benefit to the society for every extra unit of production. It exists when there is positive externality.

- Point of social efficiency occurs when $MPC = MSB$.

- Social welfare loss is the gray area in the graph. It is due to the inefficiency as quantity Q_f being produced is less than optimal quantity, Q_s.

- There are different ways to reduce social welfare loss e.g. tax exemption, subsidies etc.

Chapter 11: Resource Market

- Our discussion has been focused on product markets so far. Goods and services, that businesses produce, are only possible using **factors of production** (resources) which are land, labor, capital and entrepreneurship. These resources (factors of production) come from households.

- Firms purchase these factors of production in **factor (resource) markets**. Resources in this market are allocated in the same way as in product markets i.e. through pricing. It means greater the demand, higher the price.

- Wage is the price workers receive in return of their labor. Wage rate is the price per unit of labor.

- Depending on the number of firms buying resources, resource markets vary between extremes of **perfectly competitive** or **monopsony** markets.

Resource Demand and Supply

- Like product markets, markets for labor have demand and supply curves.

- The demand for all factors of production is a **derived demand**. It means that the demand is derived from the demand of good or service that is being produced. Greater the demand of good or service, higher the demand of factors of production.

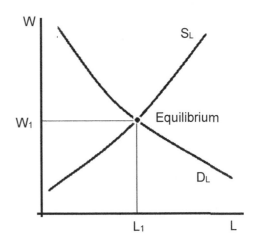

- The law of demand applies in labor market. Higher the wages, lower the demand of the labor by firms and vice versa.

- The law of supply states that higher price for labor means higher quantity of labor supply and vice versa.

Resource Demand Elasticity

- Resource Demand Elasticity is the percentage change in the quantity of labor demanded divided by the percentage change in the wages.

$$E = \frac{(\% \; change \; in \; Labor)}{(\% \; change \; in \; Wages)} = \frac{\%\Delta L}{\%\Delta W}$$

Classification of Elasticity of Demand

- Inelastic if $|E| < 1$
  It means % change in labor < % change in wage

- Elastic if $|E| > 1$
  It means % change in labor > % change in wage

- Unit Elastic if $|E| = 1$

Marginal Product and Law of Diminishing Marginal Returns

- In Chapter 03, we discussed Marginal Product and Law of Diminishing Returns.
- *Marginal Product* is the additional output that is generated when additional unit of an input is added assuming that all other inputs are kept constant.

  $$MP = \Delta Q / \Delta X$$

  ΔQ is the change in quantity of output and ΔX is the change in quantity of input i.e. productive resource (labor or capital).

- *Marginal Product of labor* is the additional output that is added with additional unit of labor.

  $$MP_L = \Delta Q / \Delta L$$

- *Law of Diminishing Marginal Returns*: The law states that in a production process if one factor of production (e.g. labor) is increased while all others are kept constant there is a point at which marginal product (*MP*) will start to decrease.
  This law applies to a firm in short run. A firm is in short run when one or more factors of production are kept constant.

Marginal Revenue Product of Labor

- Marginal Revenue Product is the change in revenue when additional unit of input is added i.e. $MRP = \Delta TR / \Delta X$

- Marginal Revenue Product of Labor is the change in revenue when additional unit of labor is added.

  $$MRP_L = \Delta TR / \Delta L$$

TR is total revenue and *L* is unit of labor.

- We know from Chapter 03, that Marginal Revenue is the change in total revenue (*TR*) per unit of quantity (*Q*).

$$Marginal\ Revenue,\ MR = \Delta TR/\Delta Q \quad => \quad \Delta TR = MR \times \Delta Q$$

- Substituting this value of ΔTR in MRP_L equation:

$$MRP_L = \frac{\Delta TR}{\Delta L} = \frac{(MR \times \Delta Q)}{\Delta L} = MR \times MP_L$$

Marginal Revenue Product of Labor (MRP_L) is equal to the product of Marginal Revenue and Marginal Product of Labor.

$$MRP_L = MR \times MP_L$$

Average and Marginal Factor Cost of Labor

- *Average Factor Cost of labor* is per unit cost of labor. It is obtained by dividing total factor cost of labor by total quantity of labor.

$$AFC_L = TFC_L/L$$

- If a firm hires all workers, *L* at the same wage, *W*; then $TFC_L = W.L$

$$AFC_L = TFC_L/\Delta L = (W.L)/L = W$$

- *Marginal Factor Cost of Labor* is the change in the labor resource cost in manufacturing a product by adding per unit labor resource. It is sometimes also known as *Marginal Resource Cost of labor* i.e. MRC_L.

$$MFC_L = \Delta TFC_L/\Delta L$$

- All firms, whether perfectly competitive or monopsony, hire resources until $\boldsymbol{MRP_L = MFC_L}$

Least Cost & Profit Maximizing Rule

- To produce maximum quantity of goods or services for a given total cost or to produce given quantity of good or service using minimum total cost, a firm needs to satisfy following condition:

$$\frac{MRP_{labor}}{MFC_{labor}} = \frac{MRP_{capital}}{MFC_{capital}} = \ldots\ldots\ldots = \frac{MRP_{land}}{MFC_{land}}$$

- Maximum profit in producing a good or service is achieved when following conditions is satisfied:

$$\frac{MRP_{labor}}{MFC_{labor}} = \frac{MRP_{capital}}{MFC_{capital}} = \ldots\ldots\ldots = \frac{MRP_{land}}{MFC_{land}} = 1$$

- It means that MRP of a resource should be equal to its MFC value.

- If the ratio of MRP to MFC is greater than 1 then more resources of that productive factor are needed.

  When the ratio of MRP to MFC is less than one then the factor of production of that particular resource needs to be reduced.

Chapter 12: Wages

- Resource markets vary between the extremes of perfectly competitive firms and monopsony firms.

Perfectly Competitive Labor Market

- In a perfectly competitive market:
    - Many relatively small firms hire workers and no firm is large enough to manipulate the market.
    - There are many workers with identical skills.
    - Both the firms and workers are wage takers i.e. no one can influence the wage rate and firms can hire as many workers as they want at the set wage rate i.e. firm's labor supply is elastic at wage rate.

- It is possible for a firm to be in perfectly competitive in labor market but not in product market and vice-versa.

MRP & MFC in a Perfectly Competitive Market

- Firms, in perfectly competitive market, hire additional workers at the same wage. This means that *MFC* and *AFC* are constants and equal to the wage rate setup by the free market.

$$MFC_L = AFC_L = W$$

- The downward sloping part of MRP_L curve is equal to the firm's resource demand curve. This is because each point represents the quantity of labor firm would hire at wage rate.

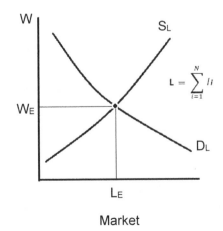

Market

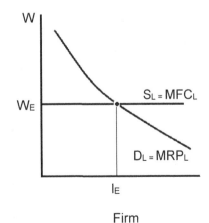

Firm

Example:

- An example below shows, how a perfectly competitive firm selling its product at a fixed given price ($5) hires labor at a fixed given wage ($100) until $MRP_L \cong MFC_L$. It has been assumed that inputs other than labor are fixed i.e. the firm is in short run. Values of labor, wage, product quantity & price have also been assumed, rest are calculated.

- Additional labor after this point (without increasing other inputs) results in negative returns.

Labor	Wage	TC (Labor)	Product Quantity	Marginal Product	Product Price	MRP (Labor)	MFC (Labor)
0	-	0	0	-	$5	-	0
1	$100	$100	150	150	$5	$750	$100
2	$100	$200	210	60	$5	$300	$100
3	$100	$300	260	50	$5	$250	$100
4	$100	$400	300	40	$5	$200	$100
5	$100	$500	330	30	$5	$150	$100
6	$100	$600	350	20	$5	$100	$100
7	$100	$700	360	10	$5	$50	$100

- Addition of new workers shift supply curve for that skill to the right. This results in decrease in the wage in industry for that skill.

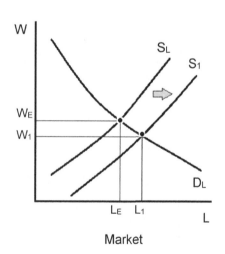

Market

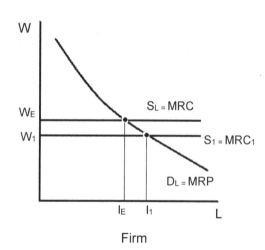

Firm

- In long run when all inputs are variable, if wage decreases, firms will be able to adjust other inputs accordingly.
- Drop in wages means that cost of production has gone down, so firms may hire more workers and increase capacity to produce more quantities.

Monopsony

- It is like monopoly except that instead of a very large seller, a very large buyer controls the market.
- In monopsony, one very large firm hires workers
- Firm is wage maker not taker

- Pure monopsony is not common. De Beers through its burying arm Central Selling Organization, CSO (which at one point bought up-to 80% of the value of diamond production) acted as monopsony.

- A single-payer government healthcare system is also an example of monopsony. Government is the only buyer of health services giving it leverage over health care providers.

Labor & Wages in Monopsony

- The supply of labor for a monopsony firm is an upward sloping curve. This curve provides the wage a firm must pay for a specific quantity of labor.

- If the firm pays all workers the same wage, the wage is same as average factor cost of labor.

- When a monopsony firm wants to hire an additional labor resource, it means that not only it will require higher wage rate for additional resource but firm will also have to give increment to all other workers already employed. This means that MFC_L is an upward sloping curve with higher slope than the supply curve.

- Monopsony firm also hires resources until $MRP_L = MFC_L$. It then determines the least cost level of employment and wages.

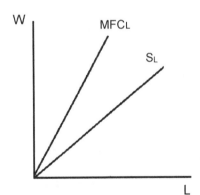 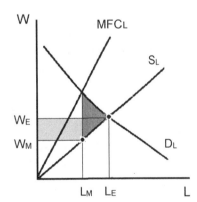

- Wages and number of labor in monopsony is less than the social optimum values in perfectly competitive firm i.e. $W_M < W_E$ & $L_M < L_E$

Minimum Wage

- Setting minimum wage and its impact has been a key point of discussion among economists.
- If minimum wage is increased in a perfectly competitive market, it may result in lesser demand and surplus supply.
- However, in a monopsony, which is closer to real-world scenario, increasing minimum wage can result in increase in both job supply and demand.

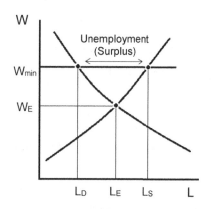

Min. Wage in Perfect Competition

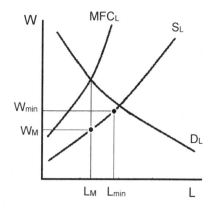

Min. Wage in Monopsony

Labor Unions

- Sometimes in resource markets, workers sell their labor services through labor unions.
- Unions work to raise wage rates for members.

Inclusive Labor Union

- It is also known as industrial labor union. It includes all workers (in an industry) in a union and demands higher wages from firms.
- Below minimum wages, these unions go on strike and do not work.

Exclusive Labor Union

- It is also known as craft labor union. In order to increase the wage rate, it restricts supply of skilled labor.
- Unions can restrict supply because in most such cases they train the skilled labor.

- Following graphs reflect impact of labor unions over supply and demand of labor. It should also be noted that:
  - The analysis has used perfectly competitive market scenario in which case setting labor unions is usually not a priority for workers.
  - Pure industrial and craft unions do not exit.

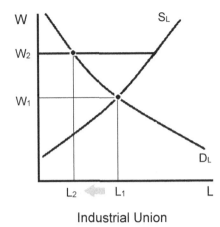

Industrial Union

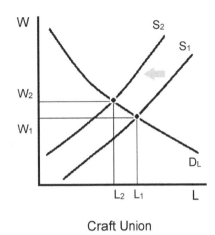

Craft Union

Bilateral Monopoly

- In imperfect markets, unions attempt to offset monopsony power by creating a monopoly on supply side. It is a complex model and is known as Bilateral Monopoly.

- Levels of new wage and labor under bilateral monopoly depend on the relative bargaining power of the firm and union.

- If all bargaining power lies with the employer, wage and labor would be W_m and L_m. If union has all the bargaining power, it would be W_{LU} and L_{LU}.

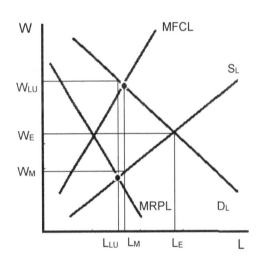

- If there is a balance between the bargaining power of both firms and labor unions, the result usually approximates competitive market and restores allocative efficiency.

Wage Differentials

- Wages paid to workers vary. Market alone is not responsible for all the variations. Wage differentials are caused by several other factors.
    - Ability, education and skill referred to as **Human Capital** is one of the most common wage differential e.g. doctors earn more than auto mechanics.
    - There may be jobs that pay more because of being hazardous or less attractive as compared to other similar jobs.
    - Geographical locations and local laws also result in wage differential.

Appendix I

Indifference Curves

- **Indifference curve** is the set of points on a graph showing different combinations of two goods between which a consumer is indifferent i.e. each point on the indifference curve has same level of utility (satisfaction) for the consumer.
- Consumer has no preference for one combination of quantity of goods over a different combination on the same curve. Therefore, indifference curves display demand patterns for individual consumers.
- A collection of the selected indifference curves is known as **indifference map**.

- Indifference curve L_1 has 2 points labeled a and b. Both these points have the same level of utility for a consumer and so does every other point on this graph.

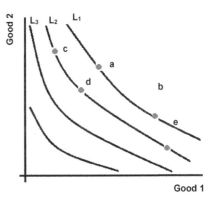

- Points c, d, e and every other point on L_2 has the same level of utility for the consumer.

- The graph L_1 represents higher utility (more satisfaction) than L_2; whereas L_4 represents least satisfaction.

Indifference Curves Characteristics

- The graphs are always negatively sloped.
- They are always either straight line or convex to the origin.
- No two curves on the graph can intersect.
- There can be infinite number of indifference curves.

Law of Diminishing Marginal Utility

- This law states that the marginal utility of a good decreases with the increase in supply (and vice versa).
  It means that as consumers use more of a product, marginal utility from each additional unit decreases.

Utility Maximizing with Indifference Curves

- People desire highest level of utility but they are limited by budget constraints.

- An example of indifference curves (X_1, X_2, X_3) is given. It is about a consumer's utility of two goods, shoes and watches. X_3 is the highest indifference curve i.e. all points (including A, B, C & D) provide greater utility than any points on X_2; whereas all points on X_2 provide greater utility than any point on X_1.

  Suppose shoes cost $40 and watch costs $200 and the budget is 800$. With this budget, customer can buy certain combinations of watches and shoes.

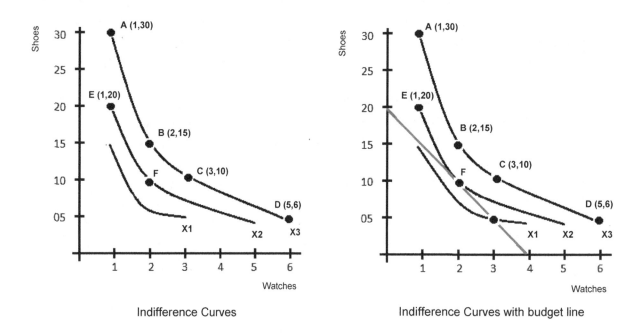

| Indifference Curves | Indifference Curves with budget line |

- Image on the right shows budget line. It is not touching X_3 at any point which means no combination on this curve is affordable due to budget constraint.

- Budget line crosses multiple indifference curves and it is always tangent to the highest possible indifference curve. It should be noted that infinite curves exist but only few are needed to find tangent point.

- In current scenario, it crosses X_1 (at point G) and is tangent to X_2 (at point F). The utility maximizing choice would therefore be point F, which means 2 watches and 10 pair of shoes would give maximum utility to this particular consumer.

Income & Indifference Curves

- Two consumers with same budget may have very different indifference curves due to different priorities.

- Increase in income or lower prices causes the budget constraint to shift right which means it becomes tangent to a higher utility indifference curve. Similarly, lower income or higher prices causes the budget constraint to shift to the left. It means it is now tangent to a lower indifference curve.

Price Change and Indifference Curves

- *Income Effect:* It means that when price of a good falls buying power rises and which price increases buying power diminishes.

- *Substitution Effect:* Substitution effect means that due to higher prices of a good, people start looking for substitutes.

- Just like indifference curves, income and substitution effect also vary among consumers.

Applications:

- Indifference curves analysis is a tool to breakdown complex consumer preferences into simpler parts.

- These curves are used in the field of rationing. Generally, commodities are rationed equally among different individuals. By considering preferences, the quantity of commodities can be measured that can help achieve a higher indifference curve and satisfaction.

- Indifference curves are also used to study preference between direct and indirect taxes. The curves show that direct tax has more satisfaction among tax payers than indirect tax.

- These curves are used to study effects of subsidy on consumers. The curves can also be helpful in measuring the cost or standard of living in terms of index numbers.

Appendix II

Basic Mathematical Concepts

Linear Equation

● For the sake of simplicity, we have assumed all relations between quantity and price to be straight lines. Equation of a straight line is a linear equation and it can be written as:

$$Y - y_1 = m\,(X - x_1)$$

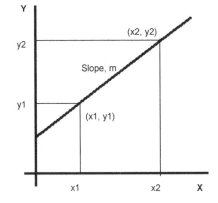

● Where Y and X are variables, m is the slope of the line and x_1, y_1 are the any two coordinates on the equation. Therefore, if the coordinates taken are (x_2, y_2), equation of the line is going to be:

$$Y - y_2 = m\,(X - x_2)$$

Any coordinates on a straight line give same equation.

Slope of Equation:

● Slope also known as gradient is the change in height (Y axis) by the change in horizontal distance i.e. rate of change (of Y with respect to X). It may be positive, negative or zero.

$$\text{Slope, } m = \frac{\Delta Y}{\Delta X}$$

● Coordinates of points a and b are (4,2) and (8,4) respectively i.e.

$$\text{Slope, } m = \frac{\Delta Y}{\Delta X} = \frac{4-2}{8-4} = \frac{2}{4} = \frac{1}{2}$$

● Slope of equation is ½. It would remain same if measured between any two points on this straight line. Slope of a straight line is a constant value.
● Equation of a straight line can then be found using any points on the line i.e.

$Y - y_1 = \frac{1}{2} (X - X_1)$

$Y - 2 = \frac{1}{2} (X-4)$

$Y - 2 = 1/2X - 2$

$Y = 1/2X$

- If we know the Y intercept of the straight line i.e. point at which the line intersects Y axis, the equation becomes simpler i.e.

  $Y = mX + b$

  where m is the slope and b is the Y intercept

- The straight line given above has Y intercept at point of origin i.e. b (Y intercept) is 0. Therefore, calculating equation using this:

  $Y = \frac{1}{2} X$

- Consider another example where one point of straight line is (6, 15) and another point is (0, 3)

  $$m = \frac{(15-3)}{(6-0)} = \frac{12}{6} = 2$$

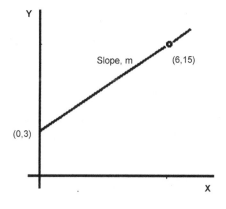

- Y intercept in this case is 3

  Equation of the line is:

  $Y = 2X + 3$

Index

Made in the USA
Middletown, DE
27 July 2022

70113923R00051